There's
More To
Running
Than
Running

Conrad Milton

First published in 2023

Cover designed by Andrew Milton and Cameron Chauhan

ISBN: 9798394477072

RRP £7.00

"Coaching is easy – only the athletes sometimes make it more difficult!"

This is written from the perspective of an endurance coach but many of the points made, and examples given, are relevant to all athletic disciplines.

1.

The Coach

Coaches come from many backgrounds but the greatest proportion have one of 3 main starting points:

a) Parents
b) Education
c) Retired Athletes

From any background, a coach may only wish to coach younger athletes before passing them on to a more senior or experienced coach whilst others will want to take them all the way – by ensuring that his/her own knowledge stays ahead of the athlete.

Parents

Parents are obviously likely to become involved through their own children. Whilst there are notable successes in the relationship with those children they are often too close to get the best results. Indeed many offspring, as they mature, see athletic development as one area of their growing independence.

A number of parents in their life will have coached few athletes other than their own children . They become gradually less involved when full independence of their offspring has occurred. Most have recognised that they will be expected to provide the 'wherewithal' until full maturity has arrived – for many this equates to passing the driving test for whilst Mum or Dad may still drive them to training they are not essential (if a car is available).

Without being told, I can usually tell the very day that the test has been successful as the change in confidence (particularly with girls) is very noticeable. The wise coach will, however, involve the parents of younger athletes by explaining what the aims are and the methods to be used to attain them. This will ensure that confidences are not broken.

Education

Educationalists will hopefully have the background knowledge and the teaching skills required to coach. But two main points remain:

1) They must allow the individual to mature and become more involved in his/her training as the years pass
2) They must not adopt a teachers stance with regards to an authority figure. Older athletes might be encouraged to write their own schedule for a limited period as their coach becomes more of an advisor.

The coach should then analyse the suggestions and point out possible defects, especially where there is a 'knock-on' effect. In any training group, discipline is required but young athletes will often start with a 'tell me what to do and I will do it' attitude. But fairly quickly this is likely to change to a coach/athlete team and eventually to a coach/

advisor relationship where the athlete is having more input to planning their progression. Each athlete is different and many will not benefit from a more scientific based approach and may even be confused by it.

Retired Athletes

Retired Athletes *can* make the best coaches but it should not be assumed (particularly by the press) that just because an athlete reached the top they can tell others how to. It was George Bernard Shaw who wisely said 'those that can do, those who can't, teach'.

To have done some running in the past helps enormously as the coach will then understand the mind of an athlete, know what is likely to motivate and thus how to get the best from an individual at any point in time. I might not have run as fast as most of the athletes I have coached, but I could always say that I had run the same type of session and knew the pain as well as the benefits; the discipline involved and the sacrifices and hardships if success was required were also understood.

However those athletes who had reached a particular level probably had a good coach but had gained experiences from race situations that few coaches would have seen at first hand. What was it like in the changing rooms at a major championship, what changed during a preparation spell abroad, what are the practicalities of altitude training, and is there a downside to warm weather work. To pass this on to the next generation is just as important as it is for the coach and athlete to discuss these experiences and learn from them where possible. Always remembering that just because something is beneficial in one country it may not work or be relevant in another because of differing social structures and pressures, for example. The athlete may not be faced with earning a living whilst abroad but has a reality check on return home. Training twice a day during a warm weather trip when a midday nap can be taken to offset tiredness is rather different from an early morning run before commencing a day's work. It is however a good introduction to this level of work.

Young athletes should be encouraged to take a medium-to-long term approach and may need to sacrifice immediate successes as an investment for the future. They should work on technique through bio-mechanical assessment and experiment with varying tactics to learn from any mistakes made.

Use of BMC-type races can be helpful, as long as competition without pacemakers is not ignored. Having a long leg length relative to an athletes body length typified many females. A powerful engine room (heart/lungs) may give endurance advantages now, but overloading may be at the expense of the speed needed to be a high level Senior. At all stages remember that legs follow the arm rate but not the reverse.

UK athletics is littered with outstanding young female athletes who have failed to hit high senior levels, often through lack of speed. Few remember the names of top youngsters but many know leading Seniors. Whilst discipline is required at all ages, it is probably most important for Seniors. One European Cross-country Champion that I previously coached did 13 sessions a week (1 weights, 1 circuits and 11 runs) and was also married, worked as a teacher 4 days a week and had a social life. Discipline and time management are *key*.

It should be noted that body-fat percentage for a female is considerably higher than that of a male. The European C.C Champion referred to above was 5ft 2 and weighed 7 stone 7lbs yet at one time had a body fat percentage of 25 + whereas a Commonwealth Games male athlete of 6ft 1 and weighing 12 stone was measured at the same time as having only 4.7%.

2.

Coach/Athlete Relationship

Whatever the background, the coach/athlete relationship is a team approach – Using the approach that 'it is you and I against the world', even when they are part of a training group.

The group is there to provide company and comradeship, but all will develop at a different rate. No one should be allowed to feel that their rightful place is at the back. Members of the group do not all need to have the same goals or have the same event as their main aim – they may have the same coach, but for each person it is a 1:1 relationship.

For his part the coach must ensure that he speaks to every member of the group each time they are together and has *no* obvious favourites. If whilst together an athlete cannot speak privately to the coach, they must make contact later.

So what are the roles of the coach and the athlete? For the latter it may seem obvious but there can be more to it:

- Agree a set of goals with the coach
- Understand what is required in building on strengths and remedying weaknesses

The coach will have his own developing philosophy whatever his/her background and the aspirations may vary from helping generally, to youth and community work, to producing international athletes. He may be a motivator or an educator (or both!). All hopefully will seek to maximise the athletes potential and the athlete should bear all of the above in mind before asking someone to coach them.

So, why have a coach?

a) To gain from another persons knowledge and/or experience
b) Comradeship/friendship
c) Sounding board for the athletes own ideas
d) Discipline: the athlete might let himself down but not another
e) Planning: the most important. It can be done by the self coached but seldom is and if not undertaken a jumble of unconnected sessions can result.
f) Guidance.

3.

Planning

Both Athlete and Coach should agree that planning will always be required. Almost certainly, things will change during the year but it is easier to deal with the unexpected by adapting a plan than to not have a plan to start with. The planning process is probably best commenced in October, at the end of the track season. At an initial one-to-one meeting, the progression sought in the coming months can be discussed and the athletes targets agreed. Note '*agreed*' – since the coach should not merely set these in isolation, as both should be working together towards the same goals.

Many things may come into the planning process but not all will be relevant or at the same time to every athlete. These may include:

Aims

There is no point having a coach and athlete who are both aiming for different things.

Finance

Can the athlete afford the essentials that are required by way of kit, club memberships, race entry fees?

Is there the option of additional costs, such as warm weather training camps?

Equipment

Is it suitable for the event or the time of year (since if wrong it may lead to injury)?

Does the athlete remember to bring right equipment or mistakenly rely on parents to bring (or clean!) it?

A pulse monitor can be useful but often to slow recovery to the required level rather than to speed up reps.

Time Availability

Are education or social demands affecting training times?

Is the best use being made of what time remains for running?

Motivation

Are the athletes aims realistic (not an Olympic gold for a young athlete, as too many subordinate goals exist)?

Would a Sports Psychologist help to manage unrealistic expectations?

Cultural

Where appropriate is regard being paid to religious beliefs (e.g Ramadan) or social pressures (e.g during a broken marraige)?

Technical

Knowledge of both the coach and athlete – Is the athlete learning and adapting? Does the coach encourage the athletes own independence?

Facilities

Are the factilities sufficient and relevant to the type of training required? The coach may believe that running ankle deep in the surf is beneficial but there is little point considering this if dealing with an inner-city based athlete.

Methods of Training

What type of training produces what result? What, at any given moment in time, does the athlete need to ensure progress either by building on strengths or removing weaknesses. Is the athlete at an age where weight training or circuits will help. Not only during spells of injury should the use of an aqua jog belt be considered.

Running in a pool using the deep end only can maintain and improve cardiovascular fitness whilst avoiding leg impact. Keep the belt tight so that water does not get between the belt and the wearers back and remember the belt is not designed to save a drowning person. The action is very similar to a normal running style but with perhaps a 'clawing back' of the legs.

Both long runs and intervals can be done holding on to the side of the pool during rest/recovery; since the water takes body temperature down recovery can be quicker. Some say that there is a boredom factor but one Marathon runner managed a 2 hour plus run in the pool in the morning followed by a further 1 hour in the afternoon.

Often Aqua sessions started when injured are continued as an alternative training form to great effect; getting 'water time' can be a problem since swimmers may find aqua joggers a nuisance and vice versa.

Characteristics of the Athlete

Is determination sufficient or are they likely to yield under pressure?

Can they think clearly and quickly in race situations and be positive?

At frequent intervals, especially after competitions, evaluation will occur.It will be seen that the coach has a heavy responsibility and in some areas is even changing the personality of his charge as well as educating him/her. After that the 'skeleton' of a first plan will have been built and the coach can then put flesh on the bones to draw up monthly schedules.

Many of the above headings will fall within the athletes lifestyle.

4.

Lifestyle

Sleep

This is almost the most important thing in an athletes development. There is little point in training long and hard but not sleeping enough to recover and achieve an adaptive response. Sleep patterns need to be regular (not going to bed at 10 one day, 2 the next, 11 on day 3). The odd late night is, of course, to be expected but you don't catch up with just one early night. The immune system is constantly being stretched to achieve recovery and athletes are often the first to catch a bug that is doing the rounds-those at school/college/University either as student or teacher are particularly vulnerable.

Alcohol

Drinking used to be related to males only but now the Ladies cannot be excluded! The temptation of the 'Uni' bar are often greatest for those being away from home for the first time and the serious athlete must overcome this diversion quickly. Some alcohol can be good but not to a level of over-indulgence.

This being so, alcohol intake can be the final straw which leads to illness or injury. One top athlete said to me when his drinking habits were raised 'its not the drink affecting me its just the regular illnesses!' He then entered into a bet with a fellow International that he would not take any alcohol for 3 months, would not eat any junk food and only eat chips if his mother cooked them. Half way through the bet the phoned the 'stakeholder' to say he was in a pub. 'Few would admit to losing a bet so honestly' came the reply. 'Oh but I haven't lost -I'm only drinking coffee' was the punch line. On removing the drink problem he suddenly had an uninterrupted training spell and knocked 25 secs off his already good personal best at 5k.

Education/Work

Athletes in education should be encouraged to keep up to date with course work as last minute cramming will impact on training often to the detriment of both studies and athletics. Most at University will have more time available than at any other time in their lives – they should manage it wisely! The same can also be said for older athletes who work and must balance the commitments associated.

5.

The Training

In middle and long distance, there can be a commonality about the early winter training as the foundation work is done until after Christmas when the 800/1500 specialists speed up quicker than those targeting 5k/10k aims. That commonality does not mean that all do the same as not all will be at the same point in their development. Those differences will be because of age, gender and race plans. Do not be tempted to assume that females do less than their male counterparts and certainly they should be encouraged to work together as far as possible learning from each others attitudes with the females becoming more positive and confident in their approach.

Similarly for younger athletes, whilst not doing the same volumes, concentrating more on speed will benefit them in their attitudes as well as the entirety of their training sessions.

As the athlete matures, volumes of training can be increased. High mileage can give a very good base ,but it is only a foundation for better quality interval work. Similarly, twice a day training can be introduced with the first session usually limited to additional steady runs since whilst the athlete is awake they may not be 'firing on all cylinders'.

The approach for those concentrating on an indoor season will vary from the above since although after a short break at the end of the outdoor track season and a spell of foundation work speed work needs to be introduced earlier. This is frequently very difficult in the UK due to weather conditions such as ice, snow and wind, which will hamper genuine speed work. Is it realistic for someone to target p.bs when only strength work has been possible in training? You certainly do not want to enter the outdoor track season feeling low, following average indoor timings.

Much of the early winter training might best be done on grass where suitable facilities (lit stretches at the side of a road, for example) exist. Another session could be the use of hills – preferably not just from bottom to top with a jog/walk back but in an undulating loop of between 2-6 minutes interspersed with 80mtr. hill sprints and later with 80mtr. strides on the flat added. This way the cross-country runner does not sub-consciously think that on reaching the top of a hill in a race they can have a brief relaxed spell. When not racing at a weekend a tempo run around 70%-80% race pace can be included sometimes split into 2 portions with the total covered at or above normal race distance.

The coach should have a good understanding of the various types of training and what each can achieve. He will then need to apply these over the number of sessions available to the athlete at each given time of the year. This application will change as the athletes fitness improves and also in relation to their race requirements.

It is as if each type is a package on a shelf and through preparing a schedule, the coach may choose any that are on offer. For example:

2 from package a) 3 from package b) and one each from c) d) and e).

Types of training will include:

a) **Steady runs:** Comfortably below race pace as an active recovery from harder, faster sessions

b) **Interval runs:** Repetitions over a set distance each done at or faster than race pace with recoveries normally half to 3 times the time of the distance run.

c) **Fartlek:** Swedish for 'speed play' where a total mileage is covered (or time spent running) with steady periods interspersed with effort, faster, phases of different distances (not normally a set number of repeats of the same distance). The emphasis can be on longer efforts in winter or shorter faster efforts in summer; in a group or squad session it can be 'nomination' fartlek with each person in turn choosing the duration without telling the remainder who must go with him/her until they slow. This is after all what might happen in a race.

d) **Long runs:** Building in length as the athlete matures; the long run gives much of the endurance required by slowly increasing the size of the heart (and increasing the number of capillaries thereby improving the supply of oxygenated blood to exercising muscle). A larger heart means each heartbeat supplies more oxygen to the muscles (provided iron levels high). Resting pulse levels will decrease and provide a greater 'expansion gap' to maximum efficiency levels (e.g a resting pulse of 70 gives a range of 110 to the upper efficiency limit of c.180 (decreasing with age) but if the resting pulse is reduced to 50 the range increases to 130). Since the capillaries are also increased the supply of oxygenated blood to the working muscle is also improved.

e) **Hills:** Many will run hills from bottom to top with a jog back recovery – in winter this is not likely to improve endurance much and does not match cross-country requirements. The body soon learns that a rest comes at the top of a hill but in cross country. the athlete has to push on with hardly a stride recovery thus a loop involving both uphill and downhill elements is recommended. Initially a double loop of 5-6 minutes duration with lminute recoveries can be considered then a mix of these with a single loop of 2 minutes in sets of 3x 1 double, 3 single x 3 or 4 with l minute between reps and 2 minutes between sets. As winter progresses the doubles are dropped and replaced by sets of singles only. After Christmas, as track season preparation approaches, a shorter hill of 1 min length can be introduced later combined with hill sprints of 80 mtrs where for the first time a jog back recovery is permitted.

The benefits of hill running should be understood:

1. Action: A powerful arm drive improves technique with leg speed following
2. High pulse work for the majority of the session
3. Weights by lifting bodyweight up a resistance
4. Endurance with warm up and warm down a high volume is involved
5. Speed: As the hill length decreases, the speed element increases
6. Psychology/mental toughness use of visualisation

f) **Tempo:** A run at 75-80% of race pace, often at less than winter race distance but not normally during a race week. This can be split into 2 sections with relatively short recovery or used to precede an interval session. Some less important races can be viewed as tempo runs with only the starters gun being the difference. A 1 or 2 mile tempo effort before a track session helps raise pulse rate so that benefits of the main session start at the beginning rather than using early reps to achieve this.

g) **Speed:** Related to the event, the introduction of fast strides during or after a long run/session can be a precursor to true speed. To achieve real speed requires longer recoveries between distances that are shorter than race length, with even greater emphasis on technique. As stated previously this element is a higher priority for the younger, developing, athlete.

h) **Weights:** Usually introduced after main growth spurts have finished with sets of two thirds of max. poundage x 6-8 reps suggested to avoid addition to body weight. Regular re-testing of maximums is required as strength gain occurs. Arm curl/leg press/lat pull/bench press/leg curl/half squats are suggested.

Often multi-gym equipment is preferred by endurance and younger athletes to avoid need for a 'spotter'. Similarly for beginners if the bar alone (free weights) is heavy enough no rings need to be added. Since availability of facilities is a vital factor a good time to start for many is when (if) they go to University. A weights circuit of 6-8 exercises alternating between the muscle groups primarily involved can be considered always concentrating on the correct technique.

i) **Circuits:** Are best not introduced at the same time as weights and should like everything else be built up regularly.

6.

Injuries

Most Coaches, over a period of time, will encounter a great variety of obstacles when training athletes, such as injuries. Most will not be medically qualified but ought to know sufficient about true athletic injuries to suggest 'first aid' to the athlete (what is done when the injury occurs is often more important than what is said by a doctor 3 days later when you have an appointment).

I said true athletic injuries since what is affecting performance may not be caused by athletics – I have known athletes whose stomach cramps have been caused by appendicitis or leg strains caused by wearing the wrong shoes (as far as athletics is concerned) to a disco.

Some injuries seem to go in spells with numerous Achilles problems followed by spells when none arise. Some featuring highly in other sports are almost unknown in athletics – For example, cruciate ligament damage is quite common in football but almost unknown in athletics.

The range and variety of injury problems is however extremely wide with some appearing once in 40 years experience and others seen regularly over the same period. The coach should know his limitations medically (as well as in other areas!) and endeavour to establish contact points within the medical profession. Treatment is simpler for those having private medical insurance (likely to be few) but even within the NHS a lot of speedy attention is possible.

High on the list of those contacts required by most coaches is a biomechanics specialist and one or more physiotherapists and an osteopath. Never be afraid to seek a second opinion especially from physios but remember that for many injuries the practitioner will have a priority list of likely causes. If treatment of the first 2 of these fail to solve the problem an alternative physiotherapist will be told what has been tried and thus will start from cause 3; if treatment for this solves the problem it does not mean he is better and if they had been consulted in the reverse order the outcome might have been the same.

7.

Easing Down

The amount of recovery time required before competition to ensure peak performance varies, not only with the individual athlete but also for specific competitions. It is useful to split races into 'training races' and 'racing races'. With little or no tapering taken for the former (often local league races), this ensures there is minimal interruption to training progression with full easing prior to major races which in a UK winter season are more usual in the New Year. Should the athletes confidence show signs of slipping (more common with younger athletes), it is always possible to cut back before a lower priority event just to show what realistic results are possible and endorse how training is going.

The Optimum

For a weekend race it is quite normal to take the Tuesday session as the last hard training day with a recovery run on Wednesday slightly less than usual length and the Thursday training cut to half or two thirds both in terms of distance and speed. There is however a need to experiment by taking slightly longer e.g 7 days and to consider the mental attitude of the athlete. Some will get worried if too extensive a period of recovery is adopted and will perform better if harder work is done even 2 days before a race. Only for the most important race, thus perhaps once or twice a year, will the longer spell be used.

Paula Fudge was the first of my charges to run on the morning of a race; note the word 'run' not 'train'. By jogging down the road for a mile she was able to fool her brain into thinking it was a day like any other thereby eliminating nerves. Those travelling to an International fixture are often best advised to jog a few miles on arrival (unless it is too late in the evening) to get rid of flight stiffness.

During the ease down and particularly when at the race venue it is important not to attempt a different routine especially as regards exercises to those done normally. Note exercises done by other athletes for later evaluation and possible incorporation in ones own warm up both in training and competition. Do not risk injury on the big day by copying someone else and using muscle groups in a way they are not prepared for.

One maxim for most 2-3 days before a race is 'you wont get any fitter with a hard session but you might get more tired' and if the athlete leaves the training track feeling that he/she could have done more then they are probably going to race relaxed and well.

8.

Psychology

Few coaches will have psychology qualifications but most, if not all, will need to be amateur psychologists if they are to get the best from those they advise. The coach/athlete relationship is based on friendship and mutual trust. Should an athlete find that the coach has lied to them, it is hard to see that trust being regained in the future.

The coach may need to know about non-athletic areas of the athletes life where they are impinging on both training and competition. Not in detail perhaps, but just that a problem exists; trust is frequently enough for the coach to be consulted on a broken marriage or a wedding cancelled. He should not make a decision on subjects such as these but can be a good listener setting out the pros and cons of a situation before the athlete independently makes a decision.

Both in training and in races, good use can be made of 'visualisation' seeking reaction to a specific rival imagined as about to overtake. In a real situation the mind has been prepared and a similar reaction may well follow.

At all times positive thinking must be encouraged. The athlete will know if they have had a poor session or a bad race so do not tell them otherwise but stress the good points that are there in any situation. One athlete inexperienced at 800mtr was told by a club official (who should have known better) during a race to lose the lead at the bell. On stopping almost dead and being knocked to the floor he could only watch as his rivals sped away. Hard to see positives? Well he was advised to learn from that experience and never to listen to advice during a race and if he did want to lose the lead to move out and let a rival through. The same mistake was never repeated.

On race days, the coach may need to calm nerves or stimulate the athlete if they are seemingly too calm. Yet, he also needs to ensure that the athlete can perform well on his/her own, since the coach will never be present at every race. It is useful on occasions not to go to an event that he could otherwise be present at, to ensure that the athlete is not over-reliant on the coach.

Always give praise since the lack of it when merited will give the impression that the coach does not care. Analyse the race seeking the athletes own views which are best not immediately after the event but the following day when they have slept on it.

The Coach can seldom create a desire to succeed but can certainly maximise any burning desire that the athlete has. For the younger athlete (and even the not so young!) study can bring mental pressures that can impinge on physical and can thus limit it. Note however that academic excellence can equal an athletic brain but may not. Some of the best athletes, the quickest thinkers in athletics terms, have not been the best academics.

9.

Diet

It would be perfectly possible to write a separate book on the subject of diet alone – indeed many excellent books and articles could be recommended! In this chapter, I will try to focus on some of the main elements but the starting point is that the human body can be likened to a Formula 1 racing car but if the athlete was that car they would not expect to go very far or very fast without the right amount or quality of fuel in the tank.

There needs to be a balance between:

    a) amount/calorie content of the diet
    b) energy demands of the lifestyle

If a) continually exceeds b) then weight gain is likely. If b) continually exceeds a) then weight loss is likely (Always assuming no underlying medical condition exists).

Energy is measured in calories and comes from food or body stores. The body needs needs energy even when sleeping; the greater the activity, the greater is the energy input required. Thus it is clear that energy demand is personal and relates to the individuals way of life.

The hardest time for an athlete in terms of diet is often during an injury when amount/calorie intake is usually maintained at pre-injury levels but energy expenditure has fallen. Should any weight gain occur during this time it should be corrected steadily and without any real dieting.

Most male athletes frequently enter their winter preparations slightly over prime racing weight, having the confidence that this will decrease as training increases. Few females have the same confidence and the coach needs to exercise caution in discussing weight with them whilst ensuring that the ethos is understood.

A top class endurance athlete running/exercising up to 13 times a week will probably need up to 3 times the calories of a sedentary individual with at least twice the % of this in carbohydrate (60-70%). There are 3 main food types and the following chart may illustrate this:

% Daily Calories	Food Type	Energy Yield (per gramme)	Food Examples
57	Carbohydrate	4 calories	Pasta
			Bread
			Sugar
			Sweets
			Potatoes
			Cakes
30	Fats	9 calories	Vegetables
			Nuts
			Oils
			Animal fats
			Dairy products

13	Proteins	4 calories	Eggs
			Milk
			Beef
			Fish
			Soya

Your requirement of between 1800 (sedentary) and up to 6000 (active top sportsman) calories per day is basically 1.5 cls per kg of bodyweight per hour for 16 hours plus lcal per kg of bodyweight for 8 hrs sleep plus 8.5 cals per kg of bodyweight per hour for specific physical activity. Thus if you weigh 50kg and do a 2 hour gym workout the calorie requirement is 2450. Apply this to the table above and it is seen that the appx. amount of each food source needed is:

Carbohydrate	57% of 2450 = 1397	= 350 grammes
Fats	30% of 2450 = 735	= 80 grammes
Protein	13% of 2450 = 318	= 80 grammes

Having provided much (most) of an endurance athletes energy during exercise the Carbohydrate reserves of the body will be depleted and within 20minutes of a session ending some should be ingested (e.g.nutrigrain bar, bagel or even jelly babies) to placate the bodies craving. Don't wait until you get home or for the next main meal. During longer sessions any water taken can have carbohydrate powder added.

In addition the diet needs to include Vitamins and Minerals which (apart from Vitamin D in small amounts) are not made within the body. Vitamins are a vital part of the enzyme systems and in the functioning of the hormonal and nervous systems. They help convert food to energy.

Fat soluble Vitamins

A fish, margarine, carrots and egg yolk
D fish oil, butter, and sunlight (particularly good for bone production)
E wheat germ and vegetable oil
K green vegetables

The water-soluble vitamins that are often lacking are:

B and C

B is vital for energy production from food and C aids oxygen transport, as well by helping with the absorption of Iron. Both can be reduced in foods through cooking and storage and some supplements may be required. Finishing a meal with a fresh Orange will help iron absorption but store most oranges in the fridge since if kept at room temperature for a week they will lose half their Vitamin C by evaporation through the skin. The athlete should not assume that a multi-vitamin tablet will provide all the iron required as most have low levels of iron for an athlete and by taking more of these too much of the other ingredients can be ingested.

Vitamin B is actually a number of different vitamins (Bl/B2/B3/B6/B12) and a range of food including cereals, brown rice, milk, eggs, liver, green leaf vegetables, fish, meat, bananas and cheese (amongst others) should be included in the diet.

Minerals

For endurance athletes Iron is in many ways the most important since it combines reversibly with oxygen which is carried around the body in haemoglobin and is released into exercising muscle thus delaying the build up of lactic acid. Iron is particularly high in red meat (lean) especially the offal meats – liver, kidney, heart, green leaf vegetables (care spinach is no higher/lower than others) many cereals, dry fruit, nuts and curry powder.

Most female athletes will have lower maximum Haemoglobin levels than males largely due to menstruation and since more females are vegetarian or do not eat red meat supplements are more frequently required. Many pregnant women after a blood test are told that they are slightly anaemic; they may well have been before pregnancy but did not have a test to confirm it! Many general dietary advisors suggest that a daily intake of 15mg of iron is sufficient but the distance athlete may well require 100mg (or more for short periods if a boost is required).

There are 5 main signs that iron levels may be low; none of them is important in isolation but 2 or more in combination merit further enquiry.

a) Broken or interrupted sleep
b) Argumentative
c) Red veins in whites of eyes almost disappear
d) Behind fingernails gets much paler than usual – not the white flecks from knocking fingers
e) Spots and pimples that are not part of usual complexion

But most important is general tiredness and the observant coach will see the athlete arriving for a session looking noticeably sleepy with half closed eyes and thereafter finding it hard to concentrate and recover from each repetition.

Calcium, Potassium, and Phosphorous are important especially during the growth phases of younger athletes as they help in bone production and in muscle activity.

Fluids

The exercising body needs a lot of fluid (mostly water) to maintain the salt and water balance in the body. Particularly when travelling abroad, bottled water is preferable since quality and similarity to what one is used to can be assured. Take care with ice abroad, since it is unlikely to come from bottled water.

As temperatures rise cramping may occur and the athlete will need to ensure that fluid intake includes the mix of body salts (not just table salt) to replace those lost through sweating. Particularly in longer events such as marathon a carbohydrate powder can be added to the drink, increasing the strength at drinks stations where possible in races to maintain energy levels beyond the typical 'wall' at, or around, 19 miles.

Use of easily carried carbohydrate gels can supplement the basic water supply. On race day take in only what you are used to; if you know in advance what drink is being provided you can experiment to make sure your body does not react unfavourably. BUT drink – or take gels – early and before you feel thirsty, to allow for absorption time.

10.

Example Training Schedules

All should remember, particularly with a growing teenage athlete, that if you do next year what you did this year, progression is less likely. Progression can, in crude terms, come from an increase in quantity, quality or a mix of each and may include the introduction of weights, circuits or twice a day sessions if time permits.

So how might this all look in practice? At this stage I must stress that any schedule should be tailor made to the individuals requirements/time commitment and no-one should merely copy sample programmes set out. I am against anyone 'selling' schedules often without even having seen the athlete; in the past I once declined to coach an International athlete based in Scotland as we would seldom if ever see each other and phone contact alone was not likely to be sufficient.

At first, a basic outline plan is suggested before the coach puts flesh on the bones. Thus an example for an 800mtr runner might be:

1. Preparation	Sept/Oct	Steady runs Long reps/hills
		1 circuit session
		Strides after 1 main session
		Drills
		1 weights
2. General conditioning Strength and endurance	Nov/Dec	Steady runs
		Long reps increasing/hills
		1 weights
		1 circuit
		Fartlek or long tempo
3. Specific conditioning Speed endurance and Elastic strength	Jan/Mch	Reps at max length and shortening+ faster short recovery
		Speed
		Competition
		Hills shorter
		Drills
		1 circuit with emphasis on strength
		Weights a little heavier
4. Speed	Apl/My	Shorter reps
		Longer recoveries
		Hills shorter and sharper
		1 circuit
		Drills
		Races often part of training and experimental
		Weights
5. Competition	June +	Fine tuning 'top ups'
		Race over/under main distance at first
		Main event at Championships and bigger meets

Example Training Schedules

All subject to constant review in light of progress, injuries etc.

Specific examples for main Middle/ Long Distance events follow:

800/1500

Winter (on grass where possible)

1.	Long run of 60-90 minutes or 2x3min undulating hill, 5x 80mtrs hill sprints all x 3
2.	Steady run 6-7 miles with few relaxed strides included
3.	1 mile tempo 2 sets of 4 x 400 1min. rests+ 3 min between sets
4.	5 miles easy
5.	600-3min rest-200-4min rest all x 2 4x100 fast strides with walk back (cut recovery time if very cold
6.	Rest or easy 4
7.	Race or 7 fartlek

Summer (on track for days 3 and 5)

1.	12 miles with 5x100 strides at end or 4 sets of 3x 300 meter hill, 6x80 metre hill sprints, 4x 80 strides on flat- all x 2
2.	5-6 miles easy
3.	800/400 x 2(3minute rests) 5 x 200 2min rests
4.	5 miles steady recovery run
5.	2-4 x 3x300 1 minute/4 minute
6.	4 easy
7.	Race or 2miles tempo/5 miles fartlek

5k/10k

Winter (on grass where possible)

1.	16-17 miles or 2 sets of (6min undulating hill loop, 2 x 3minute hill loop) l min/2 rests
2.	7-8 steady
3.	3 minute-30 seconds rest-3minute x 5 1 minute/2 or 4 sets 5x200 metres with 20 secs/2min rests
4.	6 miles recovery run
5.	1 mile tempo; 3 sets of (4x2minutes with 1 /2 minute rests} 4x30 secs fast strides
6.	Easy 5-6
7.	Race or 10 mis fartlek

Races categorised as 'training' races with little easing down or 'racing' races with full ease down.

Summer (on track for days 3 and 5)

1.	12-13 miles with 3 x 100 strides in each mile or 3 sets of 2x300 metre hill, 6x80 metre hill sprints
2.	7 miles
3.	3 or 4 sets of 600 fast/4min rest, 5x300/2 min between/4min rest 6 x 150/250 jog
4.	6 miles
5.	1 mile tempo then 12 x (3x250-50 stride then rapid acceleration into 200 fast) 150 jog recoveries + 4 minutes between sets or 10x k 90 sec rests
6.	Easy 4 miles

7.	Race or 2 x 3miles tempo with 3 min between

The Coach should be aware of the technical requirements of his events but in my experience few athletes want to know the detail as long as they have confidence in the coaches knowledge.

Marathon

Unlike other events preparation is not really affected by the seasons- though weather on race day may well alter performance. A trained athlete is likely to need up to 3 months specific training whereas a beginner will need a lot more and a slower build up.

2 weeks of basic high mileage 80-110 miles, then

1.	a) 4 hills of 6 min length, 4 hills of 3 min length	
2.	a) 4 miles	b)7
3.	a) 4 miles	b)5x2 mile 2min rests
4.	a) 4 miles	b)9
5.	a) 4 miles	b)6
6.	4 easy	
7.	Race or 5 to 10k + long warm down	
8.	a) 8 miles	b)4
9.	a)4	b)7
10.	a)4	b)2xlmile, 3x1200,4xlk,Sx800 90 sec rests
11.	a)4	b) 10
12.	a)4	b) 4x5x300 100 jog/3 min
13.	5 easy	
14.	Race 10k	

15.	10 miles Tempo	
16.	a)4	b) 6
17.	a) 4	b) 8 x 1 k 90 sec rests
18.	a) 4	b) 8
19.	a) 4	b) 7 fartlek
20.	a) 4	4
21.	Race ½ Marathon or 12 with faster last 3 miles	
22.	19 miles if no race or 2x5 miles with 4 min between	
23.	a 4	b)8
24.	a) 4	b)2miles tempo, 3x5x300 100 jog/ 3 min/1 mile tempo/ 5x80 strides
25.	a)4	b)8
26.	3x800/6x400 with l min rests, 2 miles, 6x200 lmin rests	
27.	Rest	
28.	Race 10 miles	
29.	a)15 miles steady	b) 4
30.	a) 4	b) 2x2miles with 2min rest, 2x400 l min rests then repeat all
31.	a) 4	b) 6
32.	4 easy	
33.	a) 4	b) repeat 26.
34.	6 steady	
35.	Race ½ M to 20 miles	
36.	a) 10	b) 4
37.	a) 4	b) 11
38.	a) 4	b) repeat 31.
39.	a)4	b) 12
40.	a)4	b) 7 fartlek
41.	a) 4	b) 6 easy

42.	10 miles	
43.	21 with faster last 3	
44.	a)4	b) 7
45.	a)4	b) 6 fartlek
46.	a)4	b) 8
47.	a)4	(3x1k/4x400) x 3 2 min rests
48.	a)4	b) 7
49.	Race 1/2M-20 miles	
50.	If no race 22 miles; if race 10 steady	
51.	a)4	b)7
52.	a)4	b)4xlk, 2x800 x 3 2min rests
53.	a)4	b)6
54.	a)4	b) 5 x 2mls 2min rests
55.	a)4	b)5
56.	1200/600 x 4 lmin rests	
57.	15-16 miles	
58.	a)4	b) 7
59.	10 fartlek	
60.	a)4	b) 6
61.	a)4	b) 8 x 1 mile 2 min rests
62.	a)4	b) 6
63.	a)4	b) 8 fartlek
64.	15 miles	
65.	a)4	b) 9
66.	a)4	b) 7
67.	6 fartlek	
68.	5 steady	
69.	4 easy	
70.	Rest (+increase carbohydrate intake)	
71.	Race-Marathon	

A 'precis' background is set out in '*But First...*' by Dr. Frank Dick O.B.E when he was the B.A.F. Director of Coaching.

This should form an essential part of the background reading undertaken by the aspiring coach who should also, where possible, seek out, meet, and converse with others views ensuring that they discard those they do not see as relevant whilst developing others to meet their own coaching ethos.

Wherever links with specialists such as medical, physiotherapists, biomechanical experts and sports psychologists should be established. For steeplechasers a link with a hurdles specialist may be required.

This does not weaken the coaches role but enhances it, as he shows an open mind and a willingness to learn.

In summary a coach is likely to be a mix of:

- Colleague/friend
- Educator
- Confidente
- Medical advisor (purely on a personal experience basis)
- Psychologist
- Sounding board and more

He has a heavy responsibility with younger athletes in that he will be shaping/changing their personalities but must allow them to develop as individuals.

Next, I will reflect on a few of the many athletes I have coached over the years:

JACK LANE

The first athlete I coached at the old Feltham A.C. after my own modest running career was curtailed by serious injury was a 14 year old Jack Lane who, after finishing 2nd in the I.A.A.F Junior Cross country, went to the European Championships in 1971in Helsinki where he ran 28min 24 as number 2 over 10k to Dave Bedford. Not bad in those days and the differing standards are perhaps indicated by the fact that he ran 13min38.2 in the Southern Championships at Crystal Palace BUT DID NOT WIN! He was 2nd by 0.2s.

I owe a lot of my coaching success to Jack as he developed so well that I twice considered asking a National Coach to supervise his program. On each occasion I decided that if I read widely, studied and took coaching exams then I could stay ahead of him.

Three particular events are called to mind:

1. He was regularly beaten at school by a particular rival to whom he took a dislike; finishing in the teens in school races he decided that this rival should be behind him and almost overnight he was inside the top 3. Little physical development had occurred but the importance of mental preparation was clear.
2. Having a lower back injury he hung from a stand roof beam at the track with a bag of weights round his feet to stretch his torso and thus eliminate the problem.

3. He did two degrees (at Southampton and Birmingham) and as he transferred between the two we were not able to meet up to discuss training and spoke regularly on the phone; afterwards I could not decide if I was to prepare a schedule for the coming month for his comment or if he would suggest a program for my comments. I decided to send my thoughts and sent a 28 day schedule and the next day his thoughts arrived-the two having crossed in the post. The two versions were put side by side and only 3 days of the 28 were different-and not materially so. WE were clearly thinking alike!

At Senior level he saw Dave Bedford running 150 miles a week and since his long run had reached 30 miles, he tried this but for 1 month only as we found thereafter that he did not need to repeat this to gain the same benefits getting more from better quality interval work. As Peter Snell had stressed, the high mileage was only to improve fitness for shorter, faster, intervals.

After injury problems and now married, Jack emigrated to Australia where he set himself a target of 1000 miles in 100 days, achieving this twice before further injury ended his career. He now lives in Tasmania.

PAULA FUDGE

The other half of the Yeoman Twins Paula was more fluent than Ann but initially less aggressive – until the 1978 Commonwealth Games. Two years prior to this at our planning meeting I suggested that her weekly long run should move from 12 to 15 miles. Paula disagreed and we nearly fell out. Fortunately I decided that the intended result could be achieved in another way and although she did improve that year it was only by a modest increment.

One year later at our next review meeting, I asked what she thought was required for further improvement – 'Well, I've got to do 15 miles for my long runs, haven't I?' was the immediate reply.

Next summer at the Commonwealth Games, Paula won in 9min 13 despite the altitude of Edmonton and on an extremely windy day with Ann, they became the first twins to stand together on the victory rostrum at a major Championship. Two weeks later she finished 7th in the European Championships in 8m 48.7.

In September 1981, she was asked to help pace Greta Waitz and/ or Ingrid Christianson to establish the first World Record for 5k – the fastest at the year end was to be set as the record by the I.A.A.F. Travelling to Knarvik, Norway. She found Greta had withdrawn with flu but Paula ran 3min3 per km for 3000 mtrs before Ingrid suddenly dropped out. Andy Norman the late Promotions Officer for B.A.A.B was there shouting at Paula to keep going as she was in line for the fastest time. Another 3min 3 km followed before a final 3min 2.51 to give 15min 14.51 – It was a wait to see if anyone else could go faster before December 31st! It seemed unlikely that in the few winter weeks remaining a quality field could be assembled and so it proved to be.

In 1982 Paula had her National cross country win and later in the year took the National 10 mile road race title in 54m06. In 1985 she took her 10mile road p.b. to 53.42 in Reading just 15 months after the birth of her first daughter, Rachel.

Moving to the marathon, she ran her first in Columbus, Ohio in 1985 so that she could be out of the gaze of most press. A win in 2hrs 35.11 meant the biggest prize money of her career! When someone commented that this was not bad for one days work she pointed out that it was the result of years of work and exceeded her previous total winnings by a considerable amount.

Two years later she ran her fastest of 2hr 29.47 in Chicago in October 1987.

Paula never pushed her children into the sport but they both participated until they both married and started families. Rachel was once interrupted at home when running across the lounge, bouncing off the wall, and sprinting back. In answer to Paula's question she explained that she was doing 'reps, Mum, reps!'

Throughout, Paula, like Ann, put club loyalty high on her agenda using Southern and National Leagues as useful training races.

ANN FORD

With sister Paula, known as The Yeoman Twins, Ann started in athletics with the 80mtrs, moving slowly up distance as they grew and developed. I coached her from age 17, soon after she won the English Schools 800mtr.

A most determined and aggressive runner, Ann could not wait to compete in the 1500mtrs and then the 3000mtrs, when it came into the Ladies International programme. This happened for the Commonwealth Games in 1978 and training preparation had to assume she would get the qualifying time with little or no racing experience over the distance and few race opportunities. She duly got the standard of 9min 7 and eventually went to Edmonton as Commonwealth Record Holder at 8min 52.8 there finishing 3rd in 9min 24.

Not long before Edmonton, she had married Bernie Ford who unfortunately did not make the team. I travelled to Canada privately and arrived to find Ann most upset as she had not heard from Bernie for a week (these were the days before personal computers) – this was affecting her preparation. After the 3km Ann was surprised to be speaking to Bernie on the Terry Wogan show and Bernie stressed to his tearful wife that he had written every day – Seven letters arrived together the following day!

In the International Cross Country Championships (the precursor to the World C.C) Ann finished 4th, 7th, 4th, 7th in successive years.

After her 4th place at Chepstow, I said that I had never seen her run so well but look so bad. 'I got stitch after 800mtrs and had to run with it for the rest of the race' came the reply.

Ann had won the National C.C in 1976 and set a UK Indoor 3km record of 9min27.67. She was a key member, with Paula and Annette Roberts (fastest leg), of the Feltham A.C. team that won the National Road Relay Championships (then 3 stages) in November 1978 in Coventry with the 'B' team 2nd! All 'A' team and I 'B' set the 4 fastest times

After a 2hr36 marathon debut she found the fabled 'wall' at around 19 miles and discussed this with her yoga teacher who was also a trained hypnotherapist. 'I have never tried hypnotism with a sportsperson but we can try' came the response. A tape was made so Ann could play it regularly with a scenario where she was reaching 19 miles and was feeling a surge of relaxed energy. I was just past the Tower for London Marathon in 1988 and Ann was 80 yards behind Susan Tooby (also a twin); not being able to get to the finish in time I had to go home and run a recording from the T.V. to find the final result. As the commentator some 400 yds from where I had been standing said 'there is Ann Ford now 2nd some 80 yards ahead of Tooby' I thought I had misheard so re-ran the tape. No he was right for Ann had passed 19 miles and in no time had turned an 80 meter deficit into a lead just as the hypnotherapy tape had said and she held that for a p.b of 2hrs30.38.

Would it work for everyone? Probably not, but we were glad we tried!

The late SAM HAUGHIAN

Sam was a lovey guy and an athletes-athlete. Although he was not an academic, he did have the fastest running brain I have ever met. He was a good Junior, training well with Ben Whitby and later with (Sir) Mo Farah. In his final year at school, he was unable through illness to run in the Surrey Schools trial for the English Schools Championships and surprisingly was not picked for that race. I spoke to a selector on the phone and stressed that his trial absence was genuine and a medical certificate could be provided if required. I also pointed out that he was a potential winner and a space was found for him in the Surrey team. On the day he walked the extremely muddy course and decided of his own accord where he might launch an attack; at the start of the second lap in an 800 metre stretch he sped away from a group of 10 and into a lead that grew and grew. By race end he had a gap of 1 minute which is still, I believe, the biggest winning margin in any E.S.A.A race.

A short while later, he received his first selection for the South of England to run in France. He rang me when he got the notification to say that he would probably have to decline as he only had a 'visitors passport', which had now been withdrawn. As I could countersign passport applications/photographs, I advised him to get the forms and a photo and we could go to the Passport Office at St.James Park and get the passport while we waited. When signing the photograph, I asked Sam if he had a second Christian name – 'yes it is Sean' he replied. As some names of Irish extraction have to the non Irish unusual spellings

I asked how it was spelt. 'I don't know. I don't use it. Put down James as that's what it means'! As this would not match the visitors passport and would not be accepted I guessed that Sean was correct and we proceeded to get the full passport and he went to the race.

Like many of the same age Sam had a spell of drinking and as he was a non-driver I often picked him up on a Sunday morning for hill training.

He frequently still smelled of beer from the previous evening and regularly had minor illness problems. When I pointed out the drink problem, he initially thought the two were unconnected but I stressed that his immune system was overloaded and he had little resistance to any virus that was going the rounds. He was very friendly with 2 other leading international athletes and he entered into a bet that he would have no alcohol for 3 months and, as he was a fast food fan the only chips he was allowed were those cooked by his mum. Two months into the bet he phoned one of the friends to say he was sitting in a pub. 'That is very honest' said the friend, 'few would admit to losing a bet like that'. 'Oh I haven't lost' said Sam, I'm drinking coffee!'

At the end of the bet Sam's already good 5km best of 13m45 went to 13m26 in Italy and then to 13m19 for 5th in the Manchester Commonwealth Games. His race in Italy was arranged by Zara Hyde Peters (then endurance supremo for UK Athletics) who had to call in favours from a promoter who was flooded with African athletes running under 13m30 and did not want a 13m45 performer. 'This is just the race you want,' I told Sam. 'Yes and I might beat a few' was the reply.

On return he commented that he reached 4200mtrs in 13m22. 'How I then ran a 64 sec lap I don't know! How I then ran 60 for the final circuit, I know even less about'!

He ran in a number of World cross country races both as Junior and as a Senior and in his last Junior race in Morocco he was struck down with Salmonella poisoning and put in isolation by the team management who advised him not to run. Sam pleaded, noting that he had trained so hard and the worst that could happen would be that he dropped out. He was allowed to run and worked his way through the field to a point that with 600mtrs to go he was 14th, the leading European and still passing people, when he blacked out.

On return to UK he was immediately sent to Ashford Hospital where Salmonella was confirmed and treatment started. Some weeks later he met Dave Clarke one of the management team in Morocco and thanked him for helping him off the course on that day. 'I am grateful' said Dave 'but I wasn't there as I was back in the hotel with the Seniors'. Sam had really blacked out!

On a UKA training camp in Potchefstroom, South Africa he was on a long run and doing further than his partners he was alone in fading light when he ran into a fence post, gashing his inner thigh. It was lucky that his screams were heard by some nearby foreign campers, who rushed him to a nearby hospital where fortunately a visiting surgeon was on hand to operate commenting that if the gash had been 2cm to the side, he could not have saved his life.

A year later and back in Potchefstroom on another camp (with Sir Mo), Sam was driving back from a visit South when he was killed in a car crash. It was thought to have been caused by locals, who would run in front of a car on an unlit stretch of road, forcing the driver to swerve violently and then ransacking the vehicle.

And so, a real talent was lost.

HAYLEY YELLING

Hayley was a young athlete from Yeovil who started at the old Borough Road College (West London Institute), which fully merged with Brunel University, on a Physiotherapy course when we first met. She came down to Feltham having run 10m20 for 3km and training 5 times a week.

Within 6 months she found that the course was not for her and she recoursed to Maths at St.Mary's University Twickenham, and enjoyed the new challenges and atmosphere.

Over the years, training regularly increased and she progressed in standard. It became clear that track was not her best surface but C.C was. Only 5 ft. 2, Hayley refused to accept that this was a disadvantage, but recognised that she needed a fast stride rate to achieve real success.

By 1994, she had improved to 9m46.36 for 7th in the Southern Championships. The next January, she ran in the Southern C.C at Parliament Hill expecting a top 10 finish. On the 2nd lap, as she was moving through, the stitching on her spikes disintegrated and she walked to the tape with one shoe missing and the other having just 3 stitches holding upper and sole together. Nevertheless, her first International selection came 4 weeks later in the Ekiden Road Relay in Korea, where she was 7th fastest on her leg.

In 1996, her first European C.C saw her 34th and that encouraged her to redouble her efforts to revise her track ambitions; I had reminded her when she wanted to concentrate on 3km that this was no longer an International event and as she accepted that she was not fast enough for top level 1500's she agreed to try 5km. After a couple, she was warming up with some International C.C colleagues when one asked if she liked 5k now. 'No I can't get used to 15 laps of the track' was the answer. 'That's probably because you don't do 15 laps in a 5km' was the correct response.

Eventually she got to like 5km and even attempted her first 10km. Lying on the grass at Watford after this she looked up and asked me 'when can I do the next one?'.

Progress continued on all surfaces, both domestically and Internationally. In 2001, her fastest 3k in Cardiff (8.m58.48) showed how much the improvement was and later that year she was up to 8th in the European C.C.

In 2002, she was 4th in the Commonwealth trials 5km and missed out on selection. She attempted the 10km trial the following day (not something normally advised). Amazingly, as first England finisher, she got automatic selection and was 5th in the Commonwealth race 6 weeks later.

Shortly after her 2003 campaign, started she had her first National C.C win at Parliament Hill by a massive 99sec margin, demolishing the opposition and the confidence was high leading to 5th in European C.C in Edinburgh.

2004 saw both her greatest disappointment and her greatest success.

The 10k track qualifying standard for the Olympics was set by the I.A.A.F at 31.45 (most Olympics since have seen lower standards) and despite a p.b Hayley frustrating fell 0.14 seconds outside this and could not be selected. Whilst she recognised that a Championship track medal was unlikely it took away her Olympic dream, the massive disappointment merely strengthened her C.C. resolve, and after winning the European trial she headed for Herringsdorf in North Germany. After walking the course on the eve of the race, I asked her what she thought of the course. 'Marvellous! Just like we do every week at Virginia Water' was the reply. After attacking the hills and running strongly off the top of each , she passed me and entered the final 200m in a leading group of 4. I could only watch the final stage on the giant T.V. screen and listen to the announcer calling her name. As one rival dropped off, I was delighted that she was to get a medal – and what a medal it would be – as the final 80metres was over a muddy stretch on which sand had been laid. Not breaking stride Hayley burst clear for the magical gold!

Speaking to Jo Pavey afterwards, I indicated that of the top 4, I thought she was the likely winner as she had more basic speed. 'Oh yes, but Hayley killed us up the hills and we had nothing left' was the honest reply. Race promoters wanted her for their races the following week but Hayley saw her priorities differently as she was committed to a good friends hen night on that date.

Around this time, Hayley and Ben Whitby agreed to help a leading physiologist with his thesis by taking part in a number of tests over a 2 week period, under hospital conditions. One of the first was a basic body fat analysis done by firing a pulse into the biceps (not by callipers). Ben a 6ft 2, 12 stone, Commonwealth Games steeplechaser recorded only 4.7 against the nearly 30% for the 5ft 2 Hayley, bringing a reaction that she would immediately go on a diet. No, I said, the test does not say you are overweight just that the fat needed to be replaced by productive muscle. We checked her diet and found that she 'pigged out' on cheese. A half lb block when purchased did not get into the fridge, as it was eaten before the door opened! Two weeks later, Hayley asked for the test to be repeated and it was already down to 21%.

3 further European C.C top 10 placings followed before Hayley decided to ease training loads and semi-retire, before noticing that the next Commonwealth Games were to be in India, a country she had never visited. This prompted a belated C.C trials run in Liverpool, off only 2 weeks intensive training and a win here meant that nearly 36yrs old she would contest another Euro C.C, this time in Dublin. After leading almost all the way, a second victory (by 7 secs) resulted. I don't think two European Senior C.C gold medals has been recorded by any other UK athlete apart from Paula Radcliffe.

Alas illness prevented attendance in the Commonwealth Games.

If I had to sum up Hayley in a word, it would be 'discipline'. She built up training regularly to a point where she undertook 13 sessions a week – 11 runs, 1 weights, 1 circuit – whilst married with a husband and a house to look after, plus working 4 days a week as a maths teacher, she still had a social life. It can be done but it needs *discipline*!

SIR MO FARAH

Mo was introduced to Borough of Hounslow A.C (ex Feltham A.C.) by his P.E. master at Feltham Community College, Alan Watkinson (who was later to be best man at his wedding). Alan had quickly spotted Mo's talent at a small schools race (it is interesting to note that some years later a Governor at the College praised the Club for helping Mo be a respected member of the community since otherwise he might have become 'a tearaway'). Originally coached by Alex McGee ,he wanted to join Sam Haughian and Ben Whitby in some of their sessions with me. Alex readily agreed that he joined them once a week. At the end of that year, Alex, Mo and I agreed that he would fully move to my group.

His competitive nature was readily apparent: When Alex had suggested that he ran in a Young Athletes league race as he needed the race even though he would probably win easily, the response was 'what's the record?'. But none of us could see into the future and predict what he would achieve.

I coached him during his teen age years and through a number of injury problems that included a stress fracture. He saw a number of specialists arranged by B.A.A.B., but despite these enforced pauses in his training, he was winning major domestic races for his age. In 1999, he went to the World Youth Championships where I was team coach. After his 3km in 8min21.25, he was in the mixed zone where leading athletes in a final meet the press. As he looked bemused, I went over and asked what was wrong. 'They are all congratulating me' he said.

When I noted that he had appreciably improved his already good p.b he was still stunned. 'But I came 6th and I've never been 6th before' said Mo. Incidentally 2nd in that race was Mr.K.Bekele.

During this period, I dropped him where he was living with who I understood was his aunt, but never went inside the house. I certainly knew nothing of his subsequent revelations of trafficking and original name! Indeed his naturalisation was arranged through lawyers acting for the late Sir Eddie Kulukundis, a very good friend of British Athletics and Chairman of the Sports Aid Foundation, and they clearly knew nothing of this either.

Mo was beginning to get grant aid support and as a Senior Bank Official, I arranged his first bank account requiring both Mo and I to sign so that the money could not be misspent. This was later proven to be correct, when he returned from a short visit to his native Somalia, suggesting that he might buy some land there on which to build a house later. As the funds were for athletic use only, I mentiond that the money could not be used for this purpose, and the matter was dropped.

At one domestic C.C. race, I recall walking up a hill behind a man who commented to a friend as Mo ran by in the lead 'there goes the future of G.B middle distance running'. I didn't know the man, but how right he was!

Mo later moved to St.Mary's University in a room financed by London Marathon. But having no university entry qualifications, he continued his education at nearby Richmond College. At that time, his block did not have kitchen facilities other than a microwave in each room. So

Mo decided that he would cook a chicken, putting it on a plastic plate in the microwave, dialled up 2 hours and went out. On his return, he was surprised to see a fire engine by the block and smoke coming from the window of his room! The congealed mess found to be the cause of the fire was later used as a a still life exhibit in the Art Department.

During this time, I introduced him to his agent and he got a sponsorship, opting for a contract with larger performance bonuses rather than a higher retainer (how wise this was to prove!). In 2001/2002, shortly after placing 2nd in the European C.C in Thun and winning the UK Inter-counties he was found to have a stress fracture and could only resume training 3 months later. Yet within 2 months, he was back running an 800 p.b in a B.A.L. match, but in the same month suffered a badly gashed ankle at an open meeting at Watford which needed 7 stitches. He was soon back again with a National Junior C.C win in February 2002 followed by a AAA Indoor title.

In training, we were trying to eliminate a tendency shown by many to lengthen their stride in the finishing straight as they stretch for the line – It is much better to push your arms hard and increase leg speed. This was continued in America with Alberto Salazar, and helped him run a mile in 4m00.47 at Oxford in May 2004.

When his days at St.Marys ended, he shared a house in Teddington with many of the Kenyan athletes looked after by his Agent . He was able to learn from their training attitudes and high carbohydrate diet. Mo hated losing, even if a p.b was run. He was a quick learner and even harder trainer – all attributes that would help him gain the highest running honours by coming a double double Olympic Gold medallist.

MIKE SKINNER

Mike was, and still is, a Blackheath and Bromley athlete, when he came to the old West London Institute (now part of Brunel University) having previously received schedules at his club but seldom seeing his coach.

He won't mind me saying that to start with, he was a good domestic track athlete but not good/outstanding at International level. That was not the case on the country.

Before I knew him, he had started in the English Schools Cross Country in 264th in the youngest age group, progressing to 13th senior boy at Cheltenham in 1998. This is probably the best scenario as many top 3 at Schools level get a somewhat complacent feeling that they have arrived and made the top flight. Those finishing just below feel that with a little more hard work and dedication, they can do far more.

In all , he competed in 3 World C.C Championships and 5 European C.C, with a highest of 13th achieved in Dublin in 2009. On the way to this, he went through a stage of suffering minor illness just before a trial race. So we contacted a Sports Psychologist to see if greater mental toughness might help. In addition, I was trying to make him more positive in races rather than relying on others to eventually drop off the pace.

On leaving Uni, he worked for Pace Management to whom I had introduced Mo Farah. As they had trained and raced together before, he quickly became the main link between the Agency and Mo, a role he still fulfils to this day.

He had a most efficient running action with no upper body movement other than arm drive apparent. I used him as an example to newer, often younger, athletes who felt they were using their arms when only the shoulders were swinging. Remember legs follow the arms automatically but not the other way round!

BENEDICT WHITBY

A natural hurdler and 6ft 2 or so tall, Ben was built for steeplechase and realised early on that 90% + of the event was flat running and thus that degree of training should be geared to the flat. This might change if the athlete is awful at barrier clearance! Similarly, he knew that the barrier work needed to be done at, or close to, race pace so that approach to hurdles is not totally different to that used in races.

In training, Ben was a disciplinarian and if a group session required 60 second recoveries between each rep, he made sure that he jogged to the start line in 59/60 secs, not 60-65 like the others. If the rest were not ready, then why weren't they, was his attitude.

Winning National C.C. medals as well as success in AAA Under 20 track trials, he had already begun to benefit from International experience using strength and endurance as well as speed. At one of his Junior International Chase events against the French, he won with a really fast last lap. 'Why did you not hurdle the water jump?' asked his main French rival. 'Because I never have' replied Ben. 'You were travelling that fast you should have done' came the response.

Leading up to the Commonwealth Games in 1998, he needed to qualify at the Trials in Birmingham, but came down with flu after the heats and was really in no state to run – as this would have meant no qualification he felt he had little or nothing to lose so started. At the bell, he was out of contention. Almost closing his eyes and just going for it, he climbed to a qualifying position at the tape! It was Kuala Lumpur, here we come!

Having recovered from the flu, he went ranked in the mid 20's in the Commonwealth but as that included 17 Kenyan athletes and they – like all countries – could only have 3 runners, he was ranked higher in the race. It probably did not help however, when during training at the warm-up track, he got talking to a Kenyan athlete who politely asked what event Ben was doing. On hearing that it was the 3km Steeplechase, the Kenyan fell down laughing! For Ben, his finishing position of 7th in 8m 44.24 was a fair outcome.

In 2002, qualification for the Manchester Commonwealth Games was mere straightforward but the Kenyans dominated again and Ben's 8m40.87 was another 7th.

10.

Future Hopefuls

I could give details of several others, from Home Country Internationals to World Masters Champions, who all achieved their personal aims and gave me great satisfaction in having helped them.

Like any coach, I could also list those who might have achieved more, but who had to concentrate on earning a living to the accepted detriment of training or rightly placed love, marriage and family as a higher priority.

At least 3 of the athletes currently coached by me could earn International vests in the near future, and others have still to decide which category they fall in and thus their level of commitment. Whatever they decide, they should experience fun, enjoyment and satisfaction as they work towards personal goals. Hopefully none will fall into the 'what if' trap. Looking back after running has ended and thinking 'what if I had tried harder and really committed?' and will be able to look back with the satisfaction of having tried and got the most possible from their bodies.

The coach does not have a crystal ball and cannot predict with any certainty who will reach a particular level. He can however, provide the friendship and guidance needed for them to have every chance of success.

11.

And Finally...

In my opinion, a coach is *not* someone who, often without any formal coaching experience or qualifications, sells schedules (online or in person)to people trying to improve their fitness.

Increasingly, I am hearing of those who claim to be 'coaches', selling training schedules to multiple athletes who want to achieve very different aims, often without having met the person face-to-face or seeing them train. Recipients of these programmes would usually get a better (and cheaper!) deal by visiting their local athletics club and talking to a coach who truly understands the sport.

Club coaches, in most cases, have taken the time to 'learn the trade' and can successfully identify the requirements of each athlete individually. For example, you would not visit an unqualified doctor for medical advice, so why trust your body and athletic potential to an unqualified coach? It is not worth wasting your time and money.

For more information on finding a qualified coach or a running club, please visit: www.englandathletics.org/find-an-athletics-club/

Acknowledgements

I am forever grateful to the many athletes who, through their efforts, have helped me learn how to get the best of an athletes potential – physically and mentally. Most, if not all, remain good friends to this day and I know they all have enjoyed the journey to achieving their goals in the sport and in life.

As I once said to an athlete:

I don't mind you swearing at me during training, as long as you don't swear as you get the medal!

A really big thank you to one of my current athletes, Rebecca Elphick, for all her encouragement and guidance in assembling this book and by gathering additional material from some of my past/present athletes.

I have thoroughly enjoyed the process of writing and collating this book which is now, finally, being printed. I would like to thank all the athletes I have coached over the years in helping me to continue my involvement in a sport that I love. I hope that through my personal experiences and advice in this book, it inspires and educates those who read it.

Past and Present
Athlete Testimonies

"Where to start! I was extremely fortunate enough to meet Con through a friend of mine, who suggested coming to one of their training sessions, whilst I was at home from university. From that very training session, Con took me under his wing and had the belief in me that I didn't have in myself.

I've now been training with Con on and off for the past two years despite multiple injuries and time out from running. But I can honestly say he has supported me through it all. He doesn't just look at the times you are running but also your mental, social and physical well-being.

Throughout my injuries, Con was constantly checking up on me and making sure I was ok and that I am truly grateful for and still am – He even helped me with my university dissertation!

Now I am back training he has been more supportive than ever and has helped with every aspect of my running and it is something I will always love to do! I feel a lot more confident in my running and have felt so welcomed at WSEH by Con but also by the amazing and talented athletes and individuals that attend the club."

Farran, current WSEH athlete

"At nearly 18 years old, I decided I needed a change in a coach which is when I first approached Conrad. He was prepared to coach me but I had to clear it with my previous coach. Conrad would never 'poach' athletes and always respected other coaches.

Conrad coached me on the track over 800m, 1500m, 3000m, 5000m as well as over cross country, road and eventually the marathon – For me it was all so fulfilling! With Conrad's coaching and guidance, I achieved many goals that I hadn't thought possible including World, British and Commonwealth Records, as well as numerous medals and international vests. He attended many of the international meetings when possible and went to Edmonton, Canada for the 1978 Commonwealth Games, which was great as it was my first major games.

I was a late developer as an athlete but due to Conrad's perseverance, I was finally able to achieve my goals. Always a good listener and motivator, he got me through many rough times. Conrad was always there if any athlete needed to talk at the track or on the telephone.

Coaching both my twin and I must have been a real challenge for Conrad, but he coped. All reaping rewards and recognition for our efforts. Training was intense and a challenge but it was well worth it!

I felt very lucky and honoured to have been coached by Conrad and it's wonderful to see even today the success he is still achieving with his athletes today. Thank you for everything, Conrad."

Paula, Feltham AC athlete, 1970–1990

"Since quitting competitive athletics for several years as a teenager, the pandemic saw me reintroduce myself to running. I was encouraged to join Con's group at WSEH by family members who are both past and present athletes of his. As a coach, Con was described to me as having a relaxed approach to competing, which is exactly what I needed!

Throughout my time in the group, come rain or shine, Con has never failed to be at a session – sharing his guidance and knowledge with anyone who will listen. At times, I am not the easiest athlete to coach (due to my *persistent* complaining, injuries and health issues). However, Con has never wavered in his encouragement towards my comeback to the sport. Without Con and his fantastic training group of ladies, I didn't think I would ever enjoy training again.

In writing this, I realise that have I not only found a brilliant coach in Con, but I have also gained him as a friend – Someone who supports me in all aspects of life, far beyond the realms of athletics."

Rebecca, current WSEH athlete

"When Con started coaching me at fifteen years old, I was struggling with injuries and was close to giving up running due to the inconsistency of my training. Con taught me to enjoy sessions again by looking at my long term goals rather than my injuries. He would always remind me that being a *great* senior athlete was my aim, rather than being just a *good* junior.

Since training with Con and his senior athletes, I have learnt that hard work, determination and consistency are needed to be successful – not just talant.

Running has not only given me so many opportunities in life but I have also made great friends along the way. Con has always been there to offer his support and advice whenever I have needed it and that is something that I will always appreciate."

Blake, current WSEH athlete

"Con has not only been a great coach to me but is also a really good friend. In the six years Con has coached me, we have shared so many great memories – My favourite being country karaoke sessions on the way to training.

Con constantly supports and guides me in athletics (and has always remained undeterred by my lack of improvement). Con never fails to make me laugh, he always has a smile on his face and interesting stories to tell. I am so lucky I have Con as coach and he is definitely a friend for life!"

Juliet, current WSEH athlete

"As a young athlete, I remember training at the Feltham-based Hounslow AC. I vividly rember the winter training session being hard and the summer track sessions at Feltham Arena being fast!

Con, still actively running, would take it upon himself to run with the group on most of our long runs – which you think was a good thing for a dedicated coach to do – However, at the begining of these runs Con would not just run *with* the group, he would leave the group behind!

The start of long runs were supposed to be an opportunity to have a relaxed jog and a chat. Yet after a while, it would occur to us that after 1 or 2 miles, we could not even *see* Con anymore as he was so far out in front! Not wanting our pride to be dented by being beaten, we would have to chase him down!

Unbeknown to us at the time, he later revealed that this was simply a ploy to get us running faster and stop taking the runs too easy. (He later also revealed that on these long runs, he was running the first few miles flat out! However, every time we inevitably caught up with him, he would tie up and finish the run much slower than he had intended!)"

Elaine, Hounslow AC athlete, 1978–1990

"Having never run or been involved in athletics growing up, I had very little experience when Con started coaching me in 2008. I will be forever grateful to him for the time he has invested in me and the expertise he has shared, along with many of his amusing stories.

Before I was coached by Con, I ran my first marathon in 3 hours 26 minutes. Since being under his guidance, I ran 2 hours 57 minutes in my second marathon and have now further improved over the distance to run 2 hours 44 minutes.

As well as technical and practical guidance, Con always instills belief in my own ability and never places limits on what can be achieved. Perhaps most importantly, Con always makes the hard work fun – It's been a pleasure to have him as my coach!"

Charlotte, current WSEH athlete

My coaching relationship with Con began in October 1970 when I was nearly 18 years old. My twin sister, Paula, had decided to change coach so I wanted to change with her. I was just recovering from a badly sprained ankle picked up during a high jump competition in the summer, as a result Con suggested that I give up all the field events I had been doing for the club and concentrate on the track and cross country as that was where I would excel. How true that proved to be.

By 1974 I had qualified for the European 3000mts Championships in Rome, my first big Championships and I was rewarded with a PB time. In 1976 I finally achieved another goal winning the National Cross Country and once again qualifying for the International/World Cross Country Championships in which I represented England on 7 occasions.

All Con's schedules were written out on carbonated pages (which I still have). No computers then just good old pen pushing! Con's inspiring comments and encouragement, especially if I got injured, made the road to recovery easier. His clear explanation of the training he set enabled us to achieve our goals.

In 1978 the 3000mts was added to the Commonwealth Games in Edmonton, Canada. This was another goal to work hard for, which was never a problem, Con could always rely on me to fully commit to the training sessions he set. Unfortunately, a hip injury curtailed my training for a few weeks and with it my confidence and self-belief. The gold medal eluded me and a New Zealander separated me from my sister who won gold. All credit to Con, 2 athletes, twins at that, in the same race/championships with a medal each.

In 1985 a friend of Bernie's mentioned doing a marathon, after careful consideration I decided to have a go. By then I had 2 children and Con no longer wrote his monthly schedules for me, but was always ready to give any advice and support I needed which was a great help.

There was no altitude training, no on hand physio, dieticians or psychologists, instead all we had was a week in Spain or Portugal for mid-winter warm weather training. In the 70's and early 80's it was simply Con's careful training regime and belief in his athletes' ability that produced results.

So at the end of the day, it is many thanks Con for all my successes.

Ann, Feltham AC athlete, 1970–1990

Photos

Conrad Milton (L) Paula Fudge (C) and Ann Ford (R) before the
1972 Commonwealth Games in Christchurch, New Zealand

Conrad Milton (left side, second from back) and his athletes on the 1989 warm weather training camp in Albufeira, Portugal

Mike Skinner (L), Conrad Milton (C) and Hayley Yelling (R) at the 2005
World Cross Country Chaptionships in Saint-Galmier, France

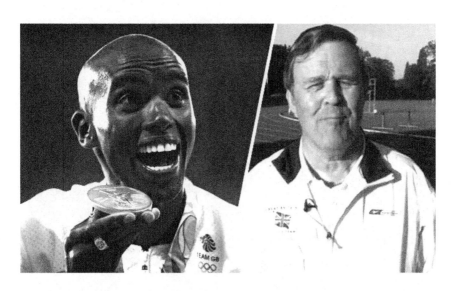

The 2016 Express news article[*] featuring Conrad Milton (R) and his
ex-athlete Sir Mo Farah (L)

[*] Online source: https://www.express.co.uk/showbiz/tv-radio/700036/Mo-Farah-coach-defends Olympics-win-gold-Good-Morning-Britain

Conrad Milton (C) and the mens WSEH team at the
2017 Chiltern League in Milton Keynes

Conrad Milton preparing to coach a winter grass session at
Upton Court Park in 2021

Conrad Milton (C) with two of his WSEH athletes at a league track race in 2021 (social distancing due to the pandemic)

Conrad Milton supprting his athletes from the stands at the
2022 British Indoor Championships at the Utilita Arena, Birmingham

About the Author

Conrad Milton has been an Athletics Coach for 56 years and during that time he has helped produce some 39 International athletes. These include winners at Commonwealth and European level and he is one of the few British coaches to count a World Record holder amongst his charges (Paula Fudge first World Record at 5000m). He coached Sir Mo Farah during his teenage years before he went to the U.S.A.

His more recent successes inc. Hayley Yelling winning the European Cross-country title twice.

On numerous occasions he acted as Team Manager or Team Coach for G.B. teams both on track, road, and country. He was National Coaching Secretary for 8 years and controlled the initial Trust Fund scheme for UK athletes receiving grants/prize money permitted within International rules. He has lectured at courses up to University level and for the training of new coaches and acted as examiner for those qualifying under the old B.A.A.B. scheme. He was Hon. Treasurer of the European Athletic Coaches Association for many years and remains a Life Vice President.

He assisted a number of schools in introducing Sports Hall Athletics and gave many lectures ranging from Physiology to Drugs in Sport and helped with their Sports days.

He was active at Club level also as Chairman of Borough of Hounslow A.C. and , having helped arrange a merger, as Deputy Chairman (to date) of Windsor Slough Eton & Hounslow A.C. helping to ensure the grass roots have the chance to develop in a healthy and disciplined way.

All of this was done as a volunteer with his career as a Bank Executive providing the integrity evidenced by friends and colleagues within the sport.